The Battle of Austerlitz

Contents

Editorial Manager: Javier Huerta
Traductions: Ronald Brighouse
English Edition: Ronald Brighaouse
Photography: Andrea Press y Ediciones Arenas
Texts: Miguel Ángel Martín Mas, Manuel Santiago Arenas y Ronald Brighouse
Lay-out: Andrea Press
ISBN: 84-96527-75-1
Depósito Legal: S. 408-2006

Edited by Andrea Press
C/ Los Talleres, 21 - Pol. ind. de Alpedrete - 28430 - Alpedrete - Madrid - España.
Tel. (+34) 91 857 00 08 - Fax (+34) 91 857 00 48 - andrea@andrea-miniatures.com
Copyright: 2006 Andrea Press

Printing: EUROPA Artes Gráficas

www.andrea-miniatures.com

Introduction

The Battle of Austerlitz is considered by many as the most brilliant of all of Napoleon's victories. It took place less than a month after the surrender of General Mack's Austrian Army at Ulm.

The Emperor had reconnoitred the field a few days before the battle, judging well where his enemies would place their troops; he predicted with great accuracy their plans. The battle itself, on the 2nd of December 1805 is the height of Napoleon's military professionalism. It clearly shows how a plan, brilliantly simple in its offensive-defensive form, executed to perfection with the right manoeuvres at the right moment can bring victory to the bold. Although he found himself in numerically inferior, he tempted his enemies into attacking him while he held a strong defensive position, and then, when his opponents had made the grave mistake of abandoning the high ground at the centre of the battlefield, Napoleon took his chance and counterattacked, dividing his enemies in two while still maintaining an adequate number of reserves to be able to influence the final outcome of the battle and then pursue his defeated enemies.

The victorious outcome for France forced the Austrians to sue for peace and sign the Treaty of Pressburg on 26th December 1805, effectively bringing the Third Coalition to an end and taking Austria out of the Napoleonic Wars until 1809.

Austerlitz is not only a great battle; we should also remember that it played an important part in the creation of the Napoleonic myth. The Napoleonic Legend, which he himself helped create, began in the days before this battle, by comparing the new Empire's rise to that of the rising sun that illuminated the battlefield where the Emperor achieved his impressive victory.

The Victory at Austerlitz was won on the first anniversary of Napoleon's coronation as Emperor of the French, and established him as the first amongst the great military leaders in Europe. In Germany this battle is called Dreikaiserschlacht, or the Battle of Three Emperors. However, it was the Emperor of the French that outshone his Austrian and Russian rivals, both in military and in political terms. Though we ought not to forget that if Napoleon had shown as much diplomatic ability as he displayed for military affairs while on campaign, the battle of Austerlitz would not have taken place and the history of Europe would have been different.

Ronald Brighouse

History of the Battle of Austerlitz

Miguel Ángel Martín Mas

Only a few hours to go before it is one year since Napoleon Bonaparte crowned himself Emperor of the French in the Cathedral of Notre Dame in Paris. The first day of December of 1805 will soon dissolve into darkness. The following morning, it is almost certain that the destiny of the audacious Corsican will be decided upon the battlefield. With him, tens of thousands of soldiers are getting ready to pass a cold night not far from a small Moravian village called Austerlitz.

Napoleon only allows himself a short rest, as his mind recalls the elegance of his coronation day. However, in an instant, his memory is also filled with images of another time, very different to the Imperial glory that was yet to arrive, Toulon, 13 Vendimiaire, the Italian and Egyptian campaigns and his proclamation as First Consul. Napoleon cannot rest, he decides he prefers the company of his soldiers rather than his memories.

It is beyond midnight when Napoleon finishes his routine inspections. An unknown soldier remembers that the 2nd December is the anniversary of the Coronation, and suddenly a cry is heard, 'Vive l'Empereur!', and it is taken up along all the French positions, and thousands of torches flare up lighting the path of the man, who, without doubt will lead them on to victory.

Before the 73,000 French soldiers there are 73,300 Austrians and 15,700 Russians. They represent the army of

Francis I (1768 - 1835)
Emperor of Austria and Holy Roman Emperor. His aunt was Marie Antoinette, Queen of France until she was guillotined during the Revolution, an act which convinced Francis to go to war against France. Disaster followed disaster, the German States lost their unity. The Holy Roman Empire ceased to exist in 1806 as a result of the formation of the Confederation of the Rhine. Following the defeats of 1805 and1809, he reached peace with France and even gave his daughter in marriage to Napoleon. In 1813 he joined the Coalition against Napoleon and helped defeat him.

Napoleon I (1769-1821)
Emperor of the French and greatest conqueror in history since Alexander the Great. He possessed imagination and ambition without bounds, as well as an inconceivable capacity to plan coupled with energy and determination. A military genius, he demonstrated his capacity to inspire his soldiers during the Italian and Egyptian campaigns. He took political power in France through a Coup D'Etat. He crowned himself Emperor in 1804. He dominated Continental Europe for years with his armies. He was defeated in 1814 by an International Coalition and was exiled to Elba. He returned in 1815 and tried to retake power, but was finally defeated at Waterloo by a British/Dutch and Prussian Army led by the Duke of Wellington and Marshall Blucher. He was exiled to the island of St Helena in the south Atlantic where he died in 1821

Alexander I (1777-1825)
Succeeded his father Tsar Paul I in 1801, following his murder. In 1805 he joins the alliance against France, but Napoleon's victory at Austerlitz meant he was unable to take part actively in European warfare untill a year later when he supported Prussia. He prevented the dismemberment of Prussia after her defeat in 1807. He cold shouldered Napoleon's proposals for marriage to a Russian princess. He opened his ports to British commerce, precipitating a war with France in 1812. In 1813 Russia led the uprising in Europe against Napoleonic power, which ended with Napoleon's fall in 1814.

The capitulation of General Mack after the Battle of Ulm. Oil painting by Charles Thévenin.

the Third Coalition, which has been formed to finish off this upstart who is threatening the stability of the thrones of Europe.

In reality, it is Napoleon himself, through his own actions, which had provoked the formation of this Coalition of forces against France and his own person. He had ordered the kidnapping and execution of the Duke of Enghein, a relative of the exiled French royal house. It was a cruel move that angered the sovereigns of Europe, and particularly Francis 1 of Austria and Alexander 1 of Russia, who joined forces with King George III of Great Britain, who had been fighting Napoleon since 1803.

Between autumn 1803 and August 1805 Napoleon had assembled a large army next to the English Channel, so determined he was to invade Britain. It was obvious, though, that to achieve such an operation he would need the cooperation of the French fleet, under the command of Admiral Villeneuve. These plans were thwarted by the Royal Navy that had blockaded his fleet in Cadiz.

Napoleon was furious when he heard of this as it meant that his invasion could not take place. However, things became even worse, as his spies in Germany informed him that Austria and Russia were assembling an army to invade France. On the 25th August 1805 Napoleon cancelled his plans for the invasion of Britain and marched his army towards Austria, intent on delivering the first blow. In under a month, the Grand Army that was supposed to be encamped by the coast in Boulogne had appeared along the Rhine and was spreading across southern Germany like a tidal wave. On the 20th October 1805, Austrian forces, numbering 27,000 men under General Mack, were surrounded and forced to surrender to Naploeon at Ulm. The following day, very far away from where the Emperor was enjoying the glory of his victory, Admiral Villeneuve lost his combined Spanish/French fleet to Nelson at the Battle of Trafalgar. This disastrous naval engagement did not stop Napoleon from continuing his campaign eastwards in search of the Russians. Amongst the infantry, some witty soldier said that the Emperor had found a new way of waging war, "he uses our legs instead of our weapons"

On the 14th November Napoleon entered Vienna in triumph. On the 19th, the cavalry vanguard under Murat occupied Brno, and for the first time in the campaign, Napoleon was facing the combined Austro Russian army. His next task was to convince the Allies that they outnumbered him and they should attack him where he wanted them to do so.

As the morning breaks on the 2nd December 1805, the frozen fields of Austerlitz will soon be soaked with blood, which men seem determined to spill century after century. The Pratzen Heights, abandoned by the French the day before to convince the enemy that their position was weak are occupied by General Kutuzov and his troops. He tries to observe the positions of his enemy, but the thick fog covers everything. He can't see them, but the Left Wing, under Marshal Lannes is on a hill named the Santon, the IVth Corps under Soult is holding the villages in the Goldbach valley, forming a wide central front that seems overextended. Davout is holding the Right Wing in the villages of Telnitz and Sokolnitz. The whole front is about 8km wide. The great numbers of Imperial Cavalry and Oudinot's Grenadiers, the Imperial Guard and I Corps under Bernadotte are held in reserve behind the Zuran heights.

On the opposite side of the valley, the Allies observe the weakness of the French Right Wing, and are convinced that victory will be theirs. The Austrian and Russian soldiers are prepared to carry out their orders once the language difficulties have been surmounted. Some 45,000 men under General Buxhöwden march forward, carrying out a large, enveloping manoeuvre to the south of the Pratzen Heights intending to cut the French line of communication to Vienna, and at the same time advance the Allied line to the Goldbach valley.

This advance is supported by 15,000 men that remain upon the Pratzen under General Krollwrath. At the same time, 17,600 men under General Bagration attack the Santon on the French left. The Russian Imperial Guard, about 8,500 men remained as a reserve in the centre, near the village of Austerlitz. This is exactly as Napoleon had hoped they would act, and the Allied High Command had no idea they were falling into a trap.

The thick fog makes the Allied advance difficult, and created confusion. However they were able to take the villages of Telnitz and Sokolnitz by 7:00 am. They are unable to do any more as Davout's men counterattack and stabilize the situation. An hour later Buxhöwden orders Krollwrath's

The Battle of Austerlitz.
Anonymous painting.

End of the battle at the ponds. Coloured engraving by J. N. Lerouge.

Napoleon with Prince Murat and Marshals Berthier, Bessières and Bernadotte dispensing final orders. Oil by Vernet.

The meeting of Napoleon and Franz I, 4 December 1805. Oil painting by Jean-Antoine Gros.

men to intervene. Napoleon, on the Zuran tries to see what is happening through the thick fog. It is around 9:00 am and it would appear the time had come to spring the trap. The Allies had abandoned the Pratzen heights to attack him, so he orders Marshal Soult to advance and take them with his two Divisions that were waiting near Puntowitz. No one on the Allied side expected such a thing and they began to wonder if the attack was simply chasing shadows in the fog. The sun that had been trying to fight its way through the mist finally manages to break through, dissipating the fog, and becoming the sign of Napoleon's Imperial Glory on that day.

It is too late for the Allies, though they try to reinforce their position on the Pratzen, so imprudently vacated to attack the allegedly weak French Right Wing. Nothing much can be done when the Corps under Marshal Bernadotte advances towards Blasowitz to reinforce Soult's left. Meanwhile around the Santon, a ferocious fight is taking place; Marshall Lannes is able to hold on to his position thanks to Marshall Murat's cavalry, who has charged repeatedly against Prince Lichtenstein's squadron to the south of the Santon. In the Goldbach valley the fight is renewed with virulent ferocity and Davout's men fall back until they are supported by Oudinot's grenadiers.

By 10:30 am, Kutuzov realises that re-taking the Pratzen is of key importance. He launches attacks on three fronts and Soult's two Divisions are hard pressed, but hold on thanks to artillery support they receive. By the time the Imperial guard reaches the heights, the fighting is all but over. But Kutuzov knows he must not lose the Pratzen, as doing so means that his left wing will be isolated. By 1:00 pm, the Russian Imperial Guard is sent forward to attack the Heights. Soult's troops start reeling before the onslaught of these giant soldiers, yet, at the last moment,

the Imperial Guard Cavalry led by Bessires intervenes, charging the Russians, forcing them to fall back, pursued by one of Bernadotte's Divisions. The centre of the battlefield is dominated by the French, so the time has come to manoeuvre and achieve checkmate, not against a King but a Tsar of Russian and an Emperor of Austria.

It is now that the Imperial Guard and what is left of Soult's troops advance to the south of the Pratzen, and envelope Buxhöwden columns which find themselves trapped between two small, frozen lakes. It is about 3:30 pm, and trying to escape the French, Buxhöwden troops attempt to cross the fragile frozen surface of the lakes, which cracks and breaks under the combined weight of men and equipment and French artillery rounds. The weight of musket balls in the cartridge boxes, the long woollen greatcoats that soak up the water, drag many men to the depths, while the remainder fight for their very survival.

Kutuzov and the Monarchs abandon the field of battle. To the north, Bagration has not been able to stop the French onslaught, and retires his exhausted men along the Olmutz road. By 4:00pm the the thunder of cannon has been replaced by the agonizing cries of the wounded.

French casualties are around 1,300 dead, 6,490 wounded and 500 missing. The Allies suffered some 16,000 dead and wounded and around 11,000 prisoners. The French nation can rejoice and forget the suffering caused by war when they see the 50 captured enemy flags that are put in display in the church of St Louis in the Invalides, Paris. The 180 guns that were captured will be melted down and a column will be made and placed in Place Vendomme.

At this moment, it is only the British that remain facing the "Ogre" Bonaparte, as his other enemies have learnt a terrible lesson from him: "It is easier to threaten me than to defeat me"

THE FRENCH ARMY

COMMANDER-IN-CHIEF: THE EMPEROR NAPOLEON - CHIEF OF STAFF. MARSHAL LOUIS ALEXANDRE BERTHIER

THE IMPERIAL GUARD
Marshal Jean Baptiste Bessiéres
5.500 men and 24 guns

INFANTRY
1st and 2nd Battalions Foot Grenadiers
1st and 2nd Battalions Light Infantry
The Grenadiers of the Royal Italian
Guard

CAVALRY
Horse Grenadiers
Light Cavalry
Mamelukes
Gendarmerie d´Elite

ARTILLERY
Light Artillery of the Guard
Artillery Train of the Guard

•

I CORPS
Marshal Jean Baptiste Bernadotte
13.000 men and 24 guns

ADVANCE GUARD
27th Light Infantry Regiment

1st DIVISION
8th Line Infantry Regiment
45th Line Infantry Regiment
54th Line Infantry Regiment

2nd DIVISION
94th Line Infantry Regiment
95th Line Infantry Regiment

LIGHT CAVALRY DIVISION
Attached to Murat's Cavalry Reserve

III CORPS
Marshal Louis Nicolas Davout
6.300 men and 9 guns

2nd DIVISION
15th Light Infantry Regiment
33th Line Infantry Regiment
48th Line Infantry Regiment
108th Line Infantry Regiment
111th Line Infantry Regiment

4th DRAGOON DIVISION
15th Dragoons Regiment
17th Dragoons Regiment
18th Dragoons Regiment
19th Dragoons Regiment
27th Dragoons Regiment

•

IV CORPS
Marshal Nicolas Jean de Dieu Soult
24.000 men and 35 guns

1st DIVISION
10th Light Infantry Regiment
14th Line Infantry Regiment
36th Line Infantry Regiment

2nd DIVISION
24th Light Infantry Regiment
4th Line Infantry Regiment
28th Line Infantry Regiment
43th Line Infantry Regiment
46th Line Infantry Regiment
55th Line Infantry Regiment
57th Line Infantry Regiment

3rd DIVISION
26th Light Infantry Regiment
3rd Line Infantry Regiment
18th Line Infantry Regiment
75th Line Infantry Regiment
Italian Light Infantry
Corsican Light Infantry

LIGHT CAVALRY DIVISION
8th Hussars Regiment
11th Light Cavalry Regiment
26th Light Cavalry Regiment

•

V CORPS
Marshal Jean Lannes
13.000 men and 40 guns

1st DIVISION
13th Light Infantry Regiment
17th Line Infantry Regiment
30th Line Infantry Regiment
51th Line Infantry Regiment
61th Line Infantry Regiment

3th DIVISION
17th Light Infantry Regiment
34th Line Infantry Regiment
40th Line Infantry Regiment
64th Line Infantry Regiment
88th Line Infantry Regiment

LIGHT CAVALRY DIVISION
9th Hussars Regiment
10th Hussars Regiment
13th Chasseurs Regiment
21th Chasseurs Regiment

GRENADIER DIVISION
General of division Nicolas Charles Oudinot
5.700 men

2nd DIVISION
Carabinier companies :
2nd Light Infantry Regiment
3rd Light Infantry Regiment
15th Light Infantry Regiment
28th Light Infantry Regiment
31th Light Infantry Regiment

Grenadier companies :
9th Line Infantry Regiment
13th Line Infantry Regiment
58th Line Infantry Regiment
81th Line Infantry Regiment

•

CAVALRY RESERVE
Marshal Joachim Murat
7.400 sabres and 36 guns

1st HEAVY CAVALRY DIVISION
1th Carabiniers Regiment
2nd Carabiniers Regiment
2nd Cuirassiers Regiment
3rd Cuirassiers Regiment
9th Cuirassiers Regiment
12th Cuirassiers Regiment

2nd HEAVY CAVALRY DIVISION
1th Cuirassiers Regiment
5th Cuirassiers Regiment
10th Cuirassiers Regiment
11th Cuirassiers Regiment

2nd DRAGOON DIVISION
3rd Dragoons Regiment
6th Dragoons Regiment
10th Dragoons Regiment
11th Dragoons Regiment
12th Dragoons Regiment
22th Dragoons Regiment

3rd DRAGOON DIVISION
5th Dragoons Regiment
8th Dragoons Regiment
12th Dragoons Regiment
16th Dragoons Regiment
21th Dragoons Regiment

LIGHT CAVALRY DIVISION
2nd Hussars Regiment
4th Hussars Regiment
5th Hussars Regiment
5th Chasseurs Regiment

LIGHT CAVALRY BRIGADE
16th Chasseurs Regiment
22th Chasseurs Regiment

•

THE ARMY TRAINS
3.000 men
3 Battalions of Artillery Train

•

TOTAL
75.000 men

THE ALLIED ARMY

NOMINAL COMMANDERS-IN-CHIEF: THE TSAR ALEXANDER I AND THE EMPEROR FRANCIS I
FIELD COMMANDER: GENERAL MIKHAIL KUTUSOV - CHIEF OF STAFF: FRANZ VON WEYROTHER

THE RUSSIAN IMPERIAL GUARD
Grand Duke Constantine
10.000 men and 40 guns

INFANTRY
Ismailowsky Guards Regiment (2 B)
Semenovsky Guards Regiment (2 B)
Preobrazhenky Regiment (2 B)
Guard Jaeger Battalion
Guard Grenadier Regiment

CAVALRY
Cuirassiers Regiment (5 S)
Cuirassiers "G. Corps" Regiment (5 S)
Lifeguard Hussars Regiment (5 S)
Cossack Lifeguard Regiment (5 S)
1 Pioners Company

•

ADVANCE GUARD OF THE TSAR´S ARMY
Lieutenant General Peter I. Bagration
14.000 men and 42 guns

INFANTRY
5th Jaeger Regiment (3 B)
6th Jaeger Regiment (3 B)
Arkhangelgorod Regiment (3 B)
5th Ingermanland Regiment (3 B)
Pskov Regiment (3 B)

CAVALRY
Empress Cuirassier Regiment (5 S)
Dragoon Tver Regiment (5 S)
St. Petesburg Dragoon Regiment (5 S)
Pavlograd Hussars Regiment (10 S)
Mariupul Hussars Regiment (10 S)
Kiselev Cosssack Regiment (5 S)
Malakhov Cossack Regiment (5 S)
Khaznenkov Cossack Regiment (5 S)

BUXHÖDEN ADVANCE GUARD
General Frederick W. Buxhöden
7.300 men and 12 guns

1st INFANTRY BRIGADE
Broder Infantry Regiment (1 B)
1st Székler Infantry Regiment (2 B)
2nd Székler Infantry Regiment (2 B)

1st CAVALRY BRIGADE **
O'Reilly Chevaulégers Regiment (8 S)
Lancers Merveldt Uhlan Regiment (1 S)
Schwarzenber Uhlan Regiment (2 S)
Hessen-Homburg Hussars Regiment (2 S)

2nd CAVALRY BRIGADE
Székler Hussars Regiment (8 S)
Cossack Sysoev Regiment (5 S)
Melentev Cossack Regiment (5 S)
Hessen-Homburg Hussars Regiment (6 S)

•

1st COLUMN
Lieutenant-General Dmitri Sergeivich Doctorov
13.500 men and y 64 guns

1st INFANTRY BRIGADE **
7th Jaeger Regiment (1 B)
N. Ingermanland infantry Regiment (3 B)
Yaroslav infantry Regiment (2 B)

2nd INFANTRY BRIGADE
Vladimir infantry Regiment (3 B)
Bryansk infantry Regiment (3 B)
Vyatka infantry Regiment (3 B)
Moscow infantry Regiment (3 B)
Kiev Grenadier Regiment (3 B)
1 Pioneers Company

ATTACHED CAVALRY
Denisov Cossack Regiment (2 S)

2nd COLUMN
Lieutenant-General A. Langeron
11.550 men and 30 guns

1ST INFANTRY BRIGADE
8th Jaeger Regiment (2 B)
Viborg Infantry Regiment (2 B)
Perm Infantry Regiment (3 B)
Kursk Infantry Regiment (3 B)

2nd INFANTRY BRIGADE
Ryazan infantry Regiment (3 B)
Fanagoria Grenadier Regiment (3 B)
1 Pioneers Company

ATTACHED CAVALRY
St. Petesburg Dragoon Regiment (2 S)
Isayen Cossack Regiment (1 S)

•

3rd COLUMN
Lieutenant-General I. Przbyswski
7.700 men and 30 guns

1st INFANTRY BRIGADE
7th Jaeger Regiment (2 B)
8th Jaeger Regiment (1 B)

2ND INFANTRY BRIGADE **
Galicia infantry Regiment (3 B)
Butyrsk infantry Regiment (3 B)
Podolia infantry Regiment (3 B)
Narva infantry Regiment (3 B)
1 Pioneers Company

•

4th COLUMN
Lieutenant-General Miloradovich and J. K. Kollowrath
23.900 men

ADVANCE GUARD
Nougorod infantry Regiment (2 B)
Apsheron infantry Regiment (1 B)
Archduke John Dragoon Regiment (2 S)

1st INFANTRY DIVISION
Nougarod Regiment (1 B)
Apsheron Regiment (2 B)
Little Russia grenadier Regiment (3 B)
Smolensk Regiment (3 B)

2nd INFANTRY BRIGADE *
Salzburgo Regiment (6 B)
Kaunitz Regiment (1 B)
Auersperg Regiment (1 B)

3rd INFANTRY BRIGADE *
Kaiser Regiment (1 B)
Czartourusky Regiment (1 B)
Reuss-Gratz Regiment (1 B)
Kerpen Regiment (1 B)
Lindeneau Regiment (1 B)
2 Vienna Jaeger Companies
2 Pioneers Companies

•

5th CAVALRY COLUMN
Prince Lichtenstein
5.375 men

1st CAVALRY BRIGADE *
Nassau Cuirassier Regiment (6 S)
Lothringen Cuirassier Regiment (6 S)

2nd CAVALRY BRIGADE *
Kaiser Cuirassier Regiment (8 S)

3rd CAVALRY BRIGADE **
Grand Duke Constantine
Uhlan Regiment (10 S)
Gordeev Cossack Regiment (5 S)
Isayev Cossack Regiment (4 S)
Denisov Cossack Regiment (2½ S)

4th CAVALRY BRIGADE
Chernigov Dragoon Regiment (5 S)
Kharkov Dragoon Regiment (5 S)
Elisabetgrad Hussars Regiment (10 S)

•

TOTAL
90.000 men and 278 guns

Russian formations but:
* Austrian formation
** Mixed formation
(B) Battalion - (S) Squadron

THE BATTLE OF AUSTERLITZ
02-12-1805

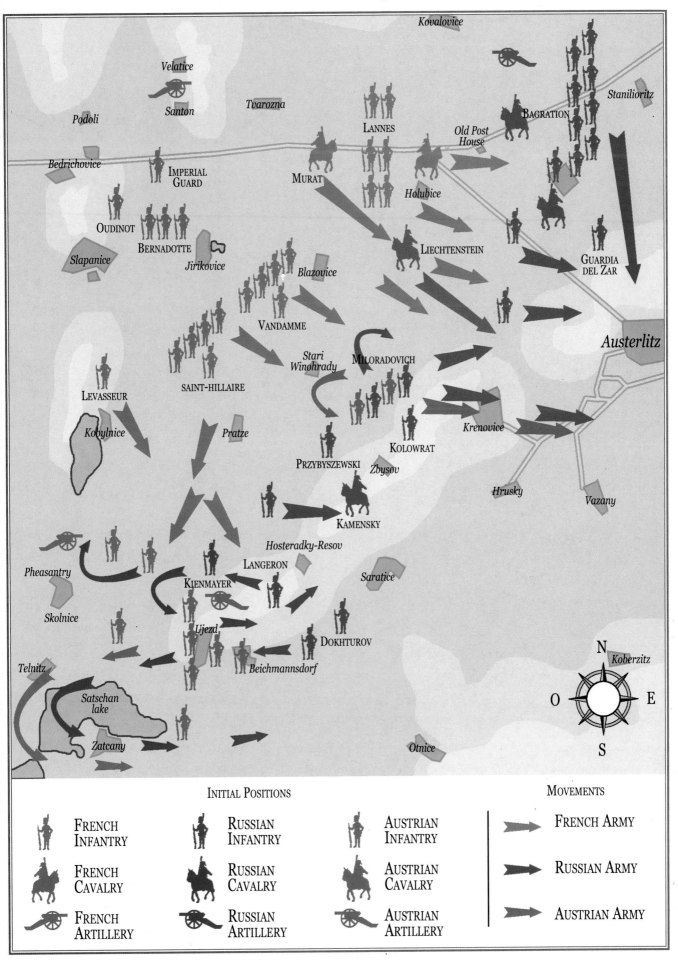

INITIAL POSITIONS | | | MOVEMENTS

FRENCH INFANTRY | RUSSIAN INFANTRY | AUSTRIAN INFANTRY | FRENCH ARMY

FRENCH CAVALRY | RUSSIAN CAVALRY | AUSTRIAN CAVALRY | RUSSIAN ARMY

FRENCH ARTILLERY | RUSSIAN ARTILLERY | AUSTRIAN ARTILLERY | AUSTRIAN ARMY

The Commemoration

Ronald Brighouse

The bicentennial commemoration and re-enactment of the Battle of Austerlitz took place from the 2nd to the 4th December 2005. The organizer's objective was to mark the anniversary of this event that brought in its wake so many political changes to Europe, as well as remember all those who died in the battle, be they soldiers from the opposing armies or the civilians who saw their villages burnt down during the battle. During these few days over 3,500 uniformed participants met in the Czech Republic to remember this historical event and all those who were present in 1805.

The historical re-enactment of the battle took place on Saturday 3rd December 2005, in a part of the original battlefield, the area known as the Santon Hill. The "Goldbach" was represented by the Tvarozna Road, and a mock village of Telnitz was built in a corner of the field. In front of the French position there was a slight elevation in the ground that would represent the Pratzen Heights. Towards the north, the "Blazovic Plains" was an area where cavalry would clash as they did 200 years ago. The Santon Hill itself became a natural grandstand for the public that naturally flocked to see the re-enactment.

The actual battle re-enactment concentrated on the fighting that took place on the French right and centre, that is the battles in Telnitz-Sokolnitz between the French Divisions of Legrand and Friant and Buxhöwden's Austro-Russian columns, as well as the main assault up the Pratzen by St Hillaire and Vandamme's Divisions, finishing with the pivoting movement by these two divisions that enveloped the Austro-Russian columns and either forced them to surrender or flee.

The battle took place on the snow covered battlefield, just as it did 200 years ago; it was as if we were back in 1805. The perception of the battle, the memories of the action are limited to what each one could see, as a re-enactment of this size usually develops smaller skirmishes within the great battle. Parts of the field were covered by a dense fog of artillery and musket smoke, these smoke clouds moved and vanished as if they were alive, sometimes covering everything with a grey blan-

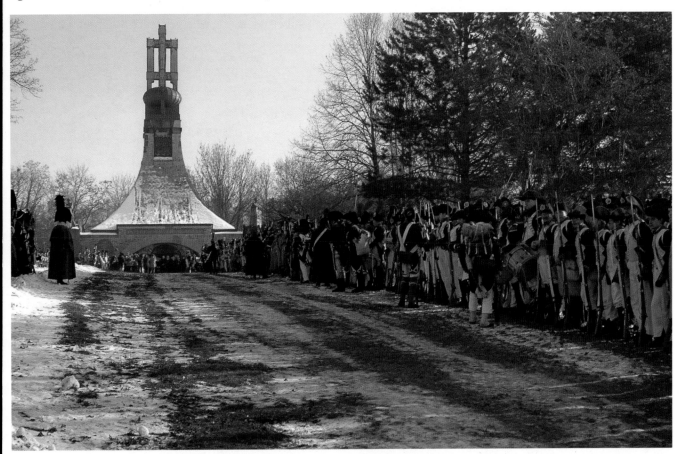

The Peace Monument on the Pratzen Heights
Left: Mark Schneider, representing the Emperor Napoleón with his ADC and Roustam, his Mameluke orderly

ket, at other times unveiling units that had advanced unseen under its protective cover. Each one of us will remember what was happening in front of our own unit, though it will be difficult to find those who had time to observe and later recall what was going on with units on either flank. Being there, and taking part in the same manoeuvres being repeated, though on a smaller scale, 200 years later, was spectacular. The memories of this re-enactment will be with each one of us who was there forever, and just like in 1805, those of us who were there in 2005 can say with pride, "Austerlitz! I was there!"

On Sunday 4th December the Commemoration Service for the fallen took place at the Peace Monument

Civil, Military and Religious Authorities during the conmemoration on the Pratzen heights

on the Pratzen. This monument was built thanks to the initiative of a local priest in Brno, Alois Slovak, (1859 – 1930), who in 1899 formed a committee whose objective was the "creation of a worthy ossuary upon the abandoned battlefield of Austerlitz". They began looking for funds to build this monument upon the Pratzen Heights. The Russian government contributed half the amount required, the Austrian and French governments also contributed funds, as did the public through donations.

The architect Josef Fanta was commissioned to design the monument, his plan was based upon a pyramid shaped Slavic tomb which rises to a height of 26 meters and includes a chapel within the building. In the chapel,

beneath a stone slab upon which the words "Peace – Honour" are inscribed, rest the mortal remains of soldiers found on the battlefield. On each corner of the pyramid there are statues representing each of the three armies that fought there, as well as an allegory of the battle itself.

The monument was built between 1910 and 1914, it was going to be inaugurated in August 1914. However the outbreak of the First World War delayed it. The monument was finally inaugurated in March 1923.

For those of us who took part in the battle re-enactment, being present at the commemoration, in uniform, remembering those who fell two hundred years ago,

Austrian Grenadiers prepare to fire a volley

Imperial Eagles parade in front of the Peace Monument

Wreath escorted by the Imperial Guard

men who wore uniforms like those we wear, is an important part of historical re-enactment. It is not simply a matter of recreating history, but also of remembering those who died there, and by learning from the mistakes of the past, avoid repeating them in the future.

There were some 2,500 persons formed on Esther side of the track that leads from the road up to the chapel in the Peace Monument. Those who represented the Emperor Napoleon, Emperor Francis and Tsar Alexander walked amongst the cheering lines of troops. Given the French victory the day before, it was obvious that the presence of Napoleon would draw from every soldier a proud cry of "Vive l'Empereur."

The service of commemoration for the dead was led by the Archbishop of Prague, Cardinal Miloslav Vlk who was accompanied by Catholic and Orthodox priests. The solemn service included prayers and hymns followed by a series of wreaths laid in the chapel by representatives of the various embassies.

Once the Service was over, each group that was pres-

ent, and so wished, was able to enter the chapel, and make a personal commemoration. Groups representing the three armies took turn in entering the chapel, forming around the central stone beneath which the remains of the old soldiers rest, and after laying a floral offering, presenting arms and holding a minute's silence, each one there honoured the fallen in a personal way.

Once the commemoration was over, the official re-enactment of the Battle of Austerlitz was over. Observing the battlefield from the Pratzen Heights, bathed in beautiful winter sunshine, it was difficult to imagine that two hundred years and two days ago, those snow covered fields were witness to such a vicious battle. Turning back to look at the Peace Monument and seeing so many representatives from different countries, all gathered here because we love history and want to remember those who died long ago. We hope to have learnt the lesson and avoid the errors of the past, working together to build a better future, creating strong links through the history we all share.

The Emperor Napoleón and his ADC's

French Soldiers in Full Dress salute the fallen in the chapel inside the Monument

Trumpeter, Horse Grenadiers of the Imperial Guard. The uniform was blue with red plastrons and turn backs, all richly decorated with gold lace.

The Battle's re-enactment

César Álvarez

Friday December 2nd 2005 saw the bi-centenary of the Battle of Austerlitz, one of the most famous and decisive clashes on the eve of modern European (World) history.

To celebrate the milestone, also called The Battle of the Three Emperors, a program of events were arranged culminating in a re-enactment of the battle on Saturday the 3rd December at Santon Hill and a service of remembrance on the Sunday at the Peace Monument.

During the first half of 2005, re-enactment groups from 24 countries were contacted and invited to take part in the event. All were registered as partner associations of the Central European Napoleonic Society (C.E.N.S), the European Napoleonic Society (E.N.S.), the Freudenkreis Lebendige Geschichte (F.L.G.), the Association Russe d'Histoire Militaire (A.R.H.M.), or organized by the Polish coordinator.

In total 3538 participants took part, of which 1981 were on the French side and 1557 on the Austro-Russian side. This was truly and international event with contingents arriving from around the globe including the United Kingdom, Belgium, Ukraine, Poland, Belarus, Netherlands, Austria and Slovakia. There were even groups and individuals from Lithuania, Latvia, Malta, Spain, Luxemburg, Switzerland, Norway, Sweden, USA and Australia. Such was the level of interest in this bi-centennial celebration that groups of re-enactors began arriving at the event site as early as Thursday, December 1st.

For Napoleon's Grande Armée of 2005 there were 118 officers, 1650 NCOs and soldiers plus a further 213 camp followers. It was armed with 1062 muskets and 24 field guns, and 114 horses were under saddle. Unlike the actual battle, this time the Austro-Russian

General Vandamme's Divison prepares to assault the Pratzen Heights

French Light Infantry engages in hand-to-hand combat with Russian Grenadiers

Russian infantry watch as 'Telnitz' burns.

army was somewhat weaker with just 92 officers, 1307 NCOs and soldiers, and 158 camp followers. It was armed with 969 muskets, 28 field guns and 92 horses under saddle.

During the 90 minutes duration of the re-enactment of the battle on the Saturday, around one ton of black powder was used. However, the paramount aspect of the whole event was the importance placed on the quality and historical accuracy of the uniforms, the training, the discipline and, above all, the authenticity of a re-enactment itself.

All the re-enactors were billeted on a military base, the capacity of which was at its maximum. There was not single place left and each barracks was bursting at the seams. While it cannot be said that the accommodation was overly comfortable, the buildings were all heated, there was an adequate number of toilets, and there was copious quantities of hot water for showers.

On Saturday morning, the units were all embarked on buses and proceeded to the battlefield without any significant delay. The cavalrymen then set about saddling their horses, the artillerymen brought up their cannons, while the infantry formed up

Austrian hussar

A clash of bayonets between French and Allied troops.

their battalions under their respective flags of one of the three Emperors.

By 13:00, everyone was ready and waiting for the initial shots to open the battle in the southern sector of the Austerlitz 2005 battlefield.

For the 2005 re-enactment, the battle was designed to show the crucial moments of the entire battle of Austerlitz just as it happened 200 years ago. The selected field under Santon Hill was the ideal setting for realising these ambitious undertakings.

The fight for Santon Hill itself could not be included in the scenario, because of the limited number of participants as well as the overall size of the battlefield.

The right wing of the French army was supposed to play the role of the Legrand and Friant Divisions from the real battle. The French

A section of Napoleon's troops ready themselves for the battle.

Remembering the fallen soldiers of the Battle of Austerlitz. On the left is the Commemorative Monument

centre was under the command of Oleg Sokolov as Marshal Soult with the cavalry reserve under the command of General John Norris as Murat. The entire army was under the command of the C.E.N.S. president, Ivan Vystrcil. In honorary command was Mark Schneider in the role of the Emperor Napoleon.

The course of the battle was that the Allied Army, under the command of Libor Fojtu, would attack with its left wing in the area of 'Telnitz-Sokolnitz'. Its 4th Column, under Alexander Gapenko, was to face Marshal Soult on the 'Pratzen Heights'. The Allied cavalry, under Alan Larsen, was to enter battle with its French counterpart in the northern sector. As soon as the Allied centre was defeated, Soult was then to bring his corps around the rear of the Allied left wing that was blocked by 'Legrand' and 'Friant' on 'Goldbach', and complete the 'victory'.

French and Austrian Infantry struggle for possession of the villages of Telnitz and Sokolnitz

French Chasseurs a Cheval support the Imperial Guard Infantry.

French Marshal accompanied by his ADC's

The 2005 Battle of Austerlitz kicked-off at 1300 with the Allied attack against 'Telnitz'. Following some impressive pyrotechnic effects by the French artillery, the divisions of 'Legrand' and later 'Friant', engulfed in clouds of gunsmoke, clashed with 'Buxhodens' columns. Despite all expectations, the French right wing probably achieved even more than in 1805, because the Allies just approached 'Telnitz' instead of assaulting. The Allied front line halted in front of 'Telnitz' instead of launching a full-scale assault, with the Allied left wing engaged in the battle. This was the moment the commander-in-chief of the Grande Armée was waiting for!

A thousand French soldiers of General (Sokolov) Soult's IVth Corps were initially hidden to the majority of the spectators in the north-western sector of the battlefield behind a reverse slope. At this point, the general received the order to advance. His battalions had to climb the opposite slope. The infantry had difficulty ascending the hill with their boots sliding on the snow, rows of men weaved about and faltered but kept going... Despite these difficulties, both the 'Saint-Hillaire' and 'Vandamme' Divisions reached the hillside of the 'Pratzen Heights' and deployed against the '4th Column'. While this may appear an easy manoeuvre on paper, in reality it was a very tough job. It must be remembered, that the IVth Corps was composed of soldiers of many nationalities participating in the battle for the first time. So, as in the actual battle 200 years ago, there were misunderstandings and mix-ups but the job got done and the battle won!

At the end of the battle, Napoleón paraded before his troops as they raised a hearty cheer for the 'victory' of their arms. The Allied troops, on the other hand, neither suffered nor mourned. With the feeling of a job well done, they lined up for the final march past and thought of the future anniversaries of Aspern, Leipzig or Waterloo where the 'winners' and 'losers' would be reversed.

Was it a successful event? The Battle of Austerlitz 2005 was unique, not only by the number of enthusiasts who had travelled from the four corners of the world to attend it, but also for the incredible level of authenticity of the re-enactment itself.

The answer can only be a unanimous 'YES'.

French Imperial Guard Grenadiers
clash with Russian Grenadiers

French Artillery supports the advancing columns of Imperial Infantry

Chasseurs à Cheval
of the Imperial Guard.

The French Army

Antonio Osende

In 1805, the French Army encamped in Boulogne, next to the English Channel, was the largest and most experienced military force in Europe. The infantry was composed of Grenadiers, Light Infantrymen and Line Infantry. The title "Regiment" which had been abolished during the Revolution was reintroduced in 1803. The French Army had 90 Line Infantry Regiments, of which 19 had four battalions and the rest had three. In March 1803 Napoleon ordered that each Light Infantry battalion was to be formed of 10 companies, of which 8 would be Chasseurs, one Carabineers and one Voltigeurs. Each Line Infantry battalion would have a Grenadier company and eight Fusilier companies. Each company would have three officers and around 80 soldiers as peace-time establishment and 123 soldiers when the country was at war. This meant that a battalion during peacetime numbered some 700 men, yet at war it should field a force of 1,100 soldiers.

In 1804 another change was introduced to the Line Infantry, one of their fusilier companies was converted to Voltigeurs (Light Infantry). The shortest, most agile men and the best shots in the regiment were transferred to this company. While Field Officers were usually mounted on horseback, it was usual to find company officers on foot as they controlled their men on the march. The French Infantry marched at 90 paces per minute, each pace around 65cm in length. The "Pas de Charge" or charging pace was only executed on the battlefield when they were trying to close with the enemy at speed. Napoleon's Army was exceptional when it came to marching, depending on the type of terrain encountered; the infantry would march in columns of Sections (10-12 men) or column of Companies (60 – 120 men).

French Cavalry during the 1805 campaign fielded 14 regiments of heavy cavalry (2 of Carabineers and 12 of Cuirassiers), 38 regiments of Dragoons, 34 Regiments of Light Cavalry (24 of Chasseurs and 10 of Hussars). The Cuirassiers had adopted the full cuirass during the Consulate, and the Carabineers did the same in 1809. They were mounted on large, heavy horses, and wielded heavy, straight bladed swords. They were used for shock tactics on the battlefield. The Dragoons were mounted on smaller horses as they could also act as infantry, which is why they were issued with carbines and bayonets as well as sabres. The only difference between the Chasseurs and the Hussars was the uniform as both types of units performed the same role on the battlefield, which was to act as Light Cavalry. In battle, it was usual for cavalry to form two lines before charging.

The Artillery had been modernized just before the Revolution. There was Foot Artillery and Horse Artillery. These were all organized as companies. They had guns of 12, 8 or 4 pounds. As well as normal canon, they also had howitzers that were used to fire shells at high angles.

Each Horse Artillery gun had a team of six horses to pull it. The gunners rode their own mounts too, which would provide replacement animals for the gun team in case of casualties. The guns were 8 pounders, they had six such pieces, and two howitzers. They fired round shot, shells and canister. The ammunition was carried in the caissons that accompanied the guns, but some rounds were also carried in the ammunition box on the gun itself.

The Old guard was present at Austerlitz, though they were part of the Reserve.
The Emperor ordered the bands to remain in the center of each battalion, the Old Guard's band played
"On va leur percer le flanc" (we'll pierce their flank), a piece of music which, according to Captain Coignet,
would make anyone get up and march.

Above left: *Grenadier of the Old Guard, detail of the bearskin cap plate. Up to 1808, the top of the bearskin sported a white cross on a red background after which it was changed to a white grenade.*

Above right: *The French infantry at Austerlitz wore the felt bicorn, it was replaced by shakos in 1807.*

Below left: *Drummers tended to be young, sometimes no more than children. Their uniforms were more decorated and more expensive than their comrades. They used to wear uniforms of inverted regimental colours, with specific decorations like the wings.*

Previous page centre: *The drums and fifes played an important role in Napoleonic warfare. They transmitted ordered on the battlefield as well as accompanying the men on the march with music.*

Above left: *The Old guard had blue greatcoats, they advanced without halting despite losses in their ranks, the "Grognards", (grumblers), represented the highest concept of military life according to the Emperor.*

Below right: *French drums were frequently damaged on campaign, as they were used to mark time on the march as well as guide the unit in battle. The "Pas de Charge" would launch the unit at the enemy.*

Above: *A Standard bearer of the Old Guard. Next to him, a Marine of the guard, wearing the 1805 uniform. The Marines were responsible for assisting in the operations of crossing rivers and lakes by means of boats and rafts.*

Below left: *The drummers and sappers were placed at the head of a column and the regiment marched behind.*

Below right: *Line Infantry Officer. This officer is wearing a brow greatcoat, and is commanding his battalion of the 3eme Regiment of the Line. This unit fought in the village of Telnitz on the Right wing of the French Army.*

Next page, above: *The Old guard does not surrender. Abandoning their fallen on the field, they continue to advance, sweeping the enemy before them. The Grenadiers of the guard advance like a blue wall, shoulder to shoulder. The Sergeant behind the line has the task of making sure no one retires or is hesitant, he will use his bayonet or the butt of his musket to control any hesitation.*

Next page, Below: *Line Infantry Grenadiers advance against the enemy. The extreme mobility achieved by French Infantry meant that they not only dominated the battlefields when in close order, but they could also reach strategic objectives before the enemy realized what was happening.*

Above left: *The solemnity of the expression on these Grenadiers of the Old Guard reflects the solemnity of the commemoration they have just carried out in the chapel on the Pratzen Heights.*

Central: *The Line Infantry was formed of three types of soldiers, Grenadiers, the tallest and strongest men, to the right of the Battalion, the Voltigeurs, shorter men, but agile, and the Fusiliers, the majority of the troops. Each Battalion had one company of Grenadiers, and one of Voltigeurs, and four of fusiliers. In this photograph we see two fusiliers wearing the bicorn "en colonne".*

Below: *Sergeant and Corporal of the Grenadiers-Fusiliers of the Imperial Guard. They are identified by the white fringe on their epaulettes. This unit was formed in 1808.*

Next page: *A young drummer wearing a uniform of inverted colours to his comrades.*

Above left: *Tactical formations in Napoleonic times were quite complex. A cloud of Light Infantry would deploy along the front line, followed by the battalion, in a Column of Divisions, two companies wide, and four in depth. Each company would deploy in three lines at about 90 cm from each other. This meant that each battalion in column had a front of 45 meters by 20 meters depth (12 lines).*

Below and next page: *The Imperial Guard represented the essence of the military concept Napoleon envisaged. Their flags and Eagles were kept in the Emperor's quarters. Any unit that came across the Guard had to stop and present arms to them.*

Above: *A typical sign of the sapper was the beard, as well as the axe. This was the main tool of the sapper. It was kept in good condition by protecting it in a leather cover carried on the sapper's back. The leather apron was designed to help protect the uniform from getting torn or snagged while the sapper was at work.*

Below: *Wonderful reproduction of the axe. The Napoleonic 'N' is engraved on the blade. This tool was also an efficient weapon when the need arose.*

Left: *The sappers had the privilege of marching at the head of their battalions. The post of honour was earned by their dangerous and hard work while leading the way into breaches or making a path for their comrades through obstacles, many times under enemy fire.*

Above: *Imperial Guard Chasseurs a Cheval officer wearing a "manteau de campagne". This coat was introduced by the Order of the 20th Pluviose in the year XII (10th February 1804). In Austerlitz, during the night before the battle, while the Chasseurs a Cheval of the Guard escorted the Emperor, they were protected from the bitter cold by clothing similar to that in the photograph.*

Below: *The Chasseurs a Cheval de la Garde had the privilege of escorting the Emperor every time he rode. They also escorted his carriage when he made use of it. When the Emperor dismounted, they also dismounted, surrounding him while he walked.*

Next page: *Line Infantry "Chef de Bataillón". On campaign, if conditions allowed it, Field Officers would try to march and fight on horseback. Only company officers would be on foot, guiding their men in battle. It is obvious that being mounted at the head of a column of men made the officer vulnerable, as he was an easy target, sought out by the enemy sharpshooters. However, a code of honour existed amongst the officer Corps that prevented an officer and a gentleman from seeking refuge amongst his men.*

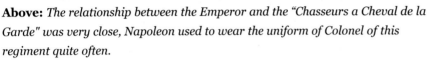

Above: *The relationship between the Emperor and the "Chasseurs a Cheval de la Garde" was very close, Napoleon used to wear the uniform of Colonel of this regiment quite often.*

Above left: *"Soldiers, I am pleased with you.....All you will have to say is I fought in Austerlitz and others will reply : " This is a brave man"...."*
(Napoleon Bonaparte, 2nd December 1805)

Centre: *To join a cuirassier regiment was not easy, the height requirement was 1.80 mts tall and have 12 years service and at least 3 campaigns. Given the stringent requirements, it is no surprise that the Imperial Army only had 12 Cuirassier Regiments*

Below: *The Cuirassiers represent the Heavy Cavalry. They were large, strong men mounted on big horses. They were considered an elite force, their role on the battlefield was the annihilation of the enemy and obtaining victory for the Emperor in the battle.*

Above left: *The Horse Grenadiers were nicknamed "the Gods" because of the pride they exuded and the way they looked down on every other regiment. The other regiments used to call them "High Heels" alluding to their height. They rode large, heavy, black horses. They wore a black bearskin cap like the Foot Grenadiers.*

Below left: *The presence of the Emperor, re-enacted very well by the American, Mark Schneider, added a touch of realism to the re-enactment of the bicentennial of the Battle of Austerlitz. In the photograph we see the Emperor's favorite uniform, that of Colonel of the Chasseurs a Cheval de la Garde, and his grey overcoat.*

Below right: *General of Brigade. The Generals of Brigades wore a gold and light blue sash. They also wore their bicorns "en colonne", that is to say, with the ends pointing fore and aft. Marshals tended to wear theirs "en bataille", that is to say with the ends pointing to the right and left.*

Above left: *This photograph shows the detail of the reproduction of the uniforms. The Chasseur a Cheval has the correct shabraque, and his sabretache is also correctly adorned. This goes to show the extent of the study into the uniformology prior to the recreation of an item.*

Above right: *Chasseur a Cheval of the Guard wearing "tenue d´escorte". While the revolutionary governments had tried to economize in uniforms and equipment, Napoleon changed all that, and tried to make his soldiers proud of their uniforms, making these spectacular and attractive.*

Centre: *Wonderful photograph of the Emperor's escort awaiting him. As in 1805, in 2005 the Chasseurs of the Guard were present.*

Below: *Chasseur a Cheval of the Guard wearing " grande tenue de service".*

Above left: *Chasseur a Cheval wearing "tenue d´route" resting by the Zuran hill. The bitter cold has made them wear their pelisses.*

Above right: *Chasseur a Cheval of the Guard. At Austerlitz in 1805, the Chasseur a Cheval of the Guard charged wearing their "grande tenue" uniforms, but many of them wore added protection to their upper body by wearing their cloak rolled as shown here, gaining a little extra protection from a sabre cut.*

Below left: *This horse bridle, richly decorated with medusa heads, as was popular at the time, indicates that this was an officer's horse.*

Below centre: *Side view of the bridle of a Chasseur a Cheval of the Guard. The Hungarian style of the Light Cavalry bridle is easily recognizable by the throat plume decoration on the horse.*

Below right: *Chasseur a Cheval of the Guard, a wonderful shot showing the saddle and equipment.*

Above: *This photograph shows the degree of uniformity that exists in this French re-enactment group.*

Next page left: *When on foot, Dragoons used black gaiters rather than their riding boots. They were equipped with a short fusil, shorter than the model 1777.*

Next page above right: *French Dragoon with greatcoat. The cape that protect the shoulders can be unbuttoned, this means the greatcoat can be worn with or without it.*

Next page centre: *Side view of a Dragoon helmet. This distinctive headgear was made from a copper alloy. There were several models, depending on the manufacturer. The chin scales helped keep the helmet on the Dragoon's head while charging, and also added protection against sabre cuts to the face.*

Next page right: *Front view of the Dragoon Helmet, note the fur turban that surrounds it. For parade the pompon was replaced by a plume the colour and length of which varied depending on the regiment and the Squadron the soldier belonged to.*

Page 39 below and 40: *The line cavalry of the Imperial Army was represented by Dragoons. When raised originally in the 18th century they were merely mounted infantry. During Napoleonic times they were used as cavalry, even though they were still given foot drill. Curiously, at Austerlitz, many units were short of horses, and were only remounted following the battle from captured Austrian and Russian horses.*

Above left: *The number of shots from each gun was usually less than that expected by the General Staff. The reason being the difficulty in obtaining replacement shot. Each gun had two or three ummunition caissons, while one was kept in reserve to the rear, the other supplied the gun in action. During the short intervals when the gun was without ammunition from the caissons the gunners used the shot carried in the gun's box, called a "Coffret". In 1801, French Artillery regulations stipulated the following ammunition issue of round shot and canister per gun:*

Gun	Shot in Box	Shot in Caisson	Canister
12 Pounds	9	48	20
8 Pounds	15	62	20
4 pounds	18	100	50
6 inch Howitzer	4	49	11

Below: *A veteran Artillery Corporal next to a Gunner, both of them wearing the "tenue de ville" corresponding to the period 1804-1806. The bicorn was replaced by the shako in 1807. The dark blue greatcoat was not introduced into the artillery till 1806, that is why in Austerlitz they fought without greatcoats or wearing whatever warm clothing they could find.*

Above right: *To be able to achieve greater mobility in battle without having to waste time limbering up the gun to the horses, the French used a system called the "bricole". By using thick ropes, some 3cm in diameter, of varying lengths, and at each end there was a leather strap which was pulled by each one of the gunners. A good example of how effective this method of moving the piece was the "charge" of the artillery by Sénarmont in Friedland, when 30 guns opened fire upon the Russians at around 1,400 meters, and then advanced by being pulled by their gun crews and firing again at 500 meters, and then at 250 meters, then 125 meters until they were firing canister into the Russian formations at 50 meters distance.*

Above: *During the Napoleonic wars artillery pieces were classified by the weight of the shot they fired rather than its caliber (internal diameter of the gun). French Artillery had guns of 4, 6, 8 and 12 pounds. French Artillery was more technologically advanced than other nations due to improvements introduced in 1766 by Jean Baptiste Gribeauval, these changes had a double purpose: the standardization of the guns, calibers and replacement parts, as well as the mobility of each individual piece, which was lacking to this time.*

Next page above: *The crew on each gun followed a specific procedure to load, aim and fire the gun. As the guns did not have any recoil shock absorbers, they had to be repositioned after each shot. The gunners would then worm the piece to remove any pieces of the cartridge left in the gun, and then sponge it to dampen any embers left inside. Then a new charge and shot was introduced and rammed home. Then the piece was primed by the gun captain by piercing the charge through the touchhole and then introducing a fuse. Once the aim was corrected, the linstock was applied to the fuse and the gun fired.*

Below: *Imperial Guard Foot Artillery Sergeant priming a howitzer. On his left shoulder you can observe the long service stripes, which in this case shows us this sergeant has over 15 years service. The gold stripe on his lower arm and the epaulette fringing of gold and red indicate he is an NCO.*

Below 1: *The precision in the reproduction of all items is characteristic of Napoleonic reenactment groups. In this case we see the reproduction of a bucket to dampen the sponge used to extinguish the embers inside the gun. It is a clear example of the attention to detail of the groups that attended Austerlitz 2005.*

Below 2: *The majority of French artillery pieces were bronze, (an alloy formed from 10 to 12 parts of tin to 100 of copper). During the revolutionary wars and the Consulate the guns had the letters RF for "Republique Francaise" engraved on them. During the Empire they had the "N" of Napoleon, within a laurel wreath and surmounted by a crown.*

Below 3: *The howitzers were known for firing shells and canister. The shells were hollow shot which contained a powder charge and a fuse, as it was fired, the fuse ignited and the shot was supposed to explode amongst the enemy, sending pieces of its casing flying around, butchering anyone within a 20 meter radius of the explosion. Canister shot was a tin cylinder filled with musket balls, which was used at close quarters against infantry and cavalry.*

Below 5: *This artillery piece was part of the battery the French Army took to Austerlitz 2005. All the pieces in this battery were original, some may have been at Austerlitz in 1805, and returned 200 years later!. The characteristic olive green colour is noticeable on the carriages and the wheels, it protects the wood from the inclement weather and the continual wear and tear of campaign. This particular colour was obtained, according to the 1801 regulations, by mixing 2,500 grams of yellow ochre paint with 30 grams of smoky black paint, the same one used to paint the metalwork on*

Below 4: *Eight inch bronze howitzer. An original cannon. Similar to a cannon, the howitzer is shorter and lighter, its propellant charge is smaller than a cannon, (1/12th of the weight of the shot rather than 1/3rd).*

1.

2.

3.

4.

5.

Russian infantry wore dark green uniforms, double breasted and with short tails. The trousers were white but on active service they were allowed to wear green, brown or grey.

The Russian Army

Ronald Brighouse

Military power gave Imperial Russia the strength to play an important role in European politics during this period. The Tsar, Alexander, changed many aspects of military organization, abolishing many Prussian changes introduced by his father. The Army reform he began took many years to complete but by 1812 the effects of his modernization were noticeable.

Russia in 1805 had one of the largest populations in the world, about 30 million inhabitants compared to 29 million French and 5 million Prussians. Although Russia had vast manpower resources, it could not be compared to the French army because the Russian economy and administration were weaker and could not maintain more than 400,000 regular soldiers and 100,000 irregular troops. These figures were what should in theory have been the Russian Army strength but in reality the army on active service was much smaller.

A new recruit joining up between 1793 and 1805 would serve "as long as he has strength and health", which meant he served for life. Later on this was limited to 25 years. Soldiers spent their time doing drill and training to alleviate the monotony of garrison life. The majority of infantrymen were young, uneducated peasants. The soldiers were renowned for their endurance and ability to march long distances with little food and rest.

Russian infantrymen at rest before the battle.

In 1805 the Russian Empire had 13 grenadier regiments, 24 Light Infantry regiments (Jägers) and 84 Line regiments. Each regiment had three battalions, two of which went on active service while the third remained in barracks and trained new recruits. Two regiments formed a brigade and three brigades made an Infantry Division.

Each battalion had one Grenadier and three Infantry companies. Each company was formed of two sections. Each year the Line Infantry regiments had to send 6 of their best grenadiers and 9 light infantrymen to the Imperial Guard.

Grenadiers had a special brass decoration on their cartridge boxes, a grenade spouting three flames. Line infantry had a grenade with a single flame and Guard Infantry had the Cross of St Andrew. The Jägers had their regimental number.

Previous page Above: *The Grenadiers and Light Infantrymen were selected from the entire battalion because of their strength, determination and good shooting skills. The tallest went to the Grenadiers and the shortest to the light infantry (strelki). Belonging to one of these companies exempted the soldier from corporal punishment.*

Previous page centre: *In winter the greatcoat was an essential item of uniform, it was to be found in grey or brown but it could also be green or black. The collar was red and the shoulder tabs were in the Divisional colour.*

Previous page below: *On campaign the great coat could be carried rolled up over the shoulder and fastened with a special strap. The cross belts were of white leather for the infantry and black for Jägers.*

Above: *A backpack of special design, made of black leather, was called a 'ranietz'. It was cylindrical and carried allthe soldier's personal kit.*

Centre right: *Infantrymen wore a black shako with white cords as decoration. Officers had silver wire cords. Line infantry had red pompons while grenadiers wore a tall, thin black plume. If the shako had a foul weather cover the company number was painted on the front with yellow paint.*

Below right an left: *The officer's uniforms were similar to the men's, but they had longer tails and were of better quality. Officers were distinguished by the epaulettes and the gorget around their collar which had the Imperial double headed eagle. A sash of silver wire with three black and orange lines was tied at the waist.*

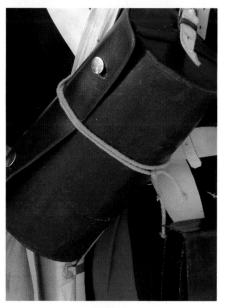

Russian officer preparing the movements of his troops.

Service in the Imperial Guard lasted 25 years. To join the Imperial Guard there was a minimum height requirement of 170cm, while in the Line Infantry it was only 155cm. Private soldiers in the Imperial Guard had equivalent rank to an NCO in the Line Infantry. Guards' Non-commissioned officers that distinguished themselves were rewarded by becoming officers in Line Regiments.

Above left: *The uniforms of the Guard were similar to the Line Infantry, but on the collar the Guardsmen had two yellow braids and on the cuffs three braids. The cartridge box sported a brass plate with the cross of St, Andrew on it and there was also four grenades, one in each corner.*

Above right: *A special order issued by the Tsar stipulated that each year, each Grenadier regiment send their 4 best grenadiers and their 2 best Jagers to St, Peterburg for induction into the Imperial Guard. This transformed the Imperial Guard into a unit composed of veterans which explains their bravery and determination in battle.*

Centre: *The Guards Officers were chosen from the nobility. They had to have education and good manners, as they were the focus of attention at Balls and other events at the Imperial Court and in Society. The Tsar insisted that all Guards Officers study the profession of arms, and he would not accept anyone that could not prove it with a certificate from the Cadet Corps.*

Below: *The Guard Jägers fought in the village of Blazowitz, and there they proved to be tenacious fighters, forcing a French column to fall back after a heated exchange of volleys.*

Russian Line Cavalry was formed of Dragoons, Light Dragoons, Uhlans (lancers), Hussars and Cuirassiers. There were 66 regiments in total. Each regiment had 6 squadrons, each squadron was formed of 125 troopers. However, the reality of campaigning meant that regiments varied in numbers between 2 and 6 squadrons.

The Dragoons were armed with carbines and a straight bladed sword. The Light Dragoons carried a carbine and a curved sabre. The cuirassiers had helmets and breastplates, and carried a straight bladed sword.

Above and next page: *The Uhlans had a lance 280cm long without pennants, as well as a sabre.*

Below: *the Cossack regiments were armed with a lance 245cm long, the lance tip had a steel ball about 15cm from the sharpened point to make it easier to remove the weapon from an enemy's body. Each Cossack had a traditional curved sabre, and 1 to 8 pistols. Some carried a carbine too a bow and arrows.*

The artillery was the most powerful arm of the Tsarist army. In 1805 no other European army was comparable when it came to the number of artillery pieces and equipment that moved with an army on campaign.

The artillery was very professional and the artillerymen educated and well trained by comparison to the infantry and cavalry. In 1805 Russia had one Horse Artillery regiment and 11 Foot Artillery regiments. The Horse Artillery wore green jackets with short tails, the collar and cuffs were black, the trousers white and they wore a leather helmet. On active service they wore grey overalls and carried a straight bladed sword. The Foot Artillery also wore a green jacket with short tails and black collar and cuffs. The white trouser-gaiters were in one piece. They wore a shako with a brass plate that had two crossed cannons and under this a grenade with three flames for the 1st and 2nd Brigade and a grenade with one flame for the other brigades. The cords and pompon for the shako were red.

An artillery Section was composed of two pieces under the commando of an NCO. Two sections (4 guns) made a Division. Three sections (6 guns) formed a Half Company. Two half companies (12 guns) formed a Company. Three companies (36 guns) formed an Artillery Brigade.

When deploying for battle, Russian artillery pieces were placed 100 meters in front of the Russian infantry. The intervals between the artillery pieces depended on the size of the gun and the turning circle each of them had, in case they had to retire quickly. The Russian artillerymen tended to look after their guns. The Tsar and the senior officers in his army expected the artillerymen to keep their guns in action till the last possible moment to cause as many casualties as possible to the enemy, and then to defend them with their lives.

Horse Artillery was used in a slightly more aggressive manner given its mobility, but there was only one regiment of these and thus were insufficient to make a drastic impact on the battlefield.

The main difference between the French and Russian artillery was not the quality of the guns but the manner in which they were employed in battle. Napoleon used artillery as an offensive weapon, preparing the strategic point in the enemy's battle line where he intended to pierce it with an infantry assault. The Russians on the other hand considered artillery as a defensive weapon and used it to protect their infantry and cavalry, forming powerful lines of canons that made piercing their line difficult. Russian Generals liked having a strong Reserve Artillery Park which they could rely upon to stop any flanking move made by the enemy.

Below: *Russian artillery pieces were bronze and were kept highly polished. The carriage and caissons and anything wooden were painted apple green while all metal pieces were painted black. Russian artillery had cannons and howitzers.*

The Austrian Army

Ronald Brighouse

During the Napoleonic Wars, Austria had general conscription. In 1805 service was 10 years for infantry, 12 for cavalry and 14 for artillery and engineers.

The Austro-Hungarian Army had between 300,000 and 450,000 regular troops and 100,000 and 150,000 irregular soldiers. It was the third largest army in the world and this was due to good organization as well as the large population that was under the influence of the Habsburg Crown.

Austrian soldiers were considered patient and disciplined, but they were seen as slow moving and ponderous when manoeuvering, with their greatest disadvantage being their multinationality. The Army had German Regiments composed of Germans, Bohemians, Moravians, and Tyroleans; the Hungarian Regiments included Hungarians, Bosniaks, Croats, and Transylvanians. There were also Italian and Wallonian Regiments and within these units there were Poles, Ukrainians, Czechs, and Rumanians.

The Austrian Officer Corps received formal instruction in Military Academies for infantry, cavalry and artillery. There were three ways of reaching officer rank, one could be made a Cadet, or purchase a commission (the preferred route for aristocrats), or earn promotion from the ranks by merit. The Cadets were the largest group of officers, and they received their instruction from the sergeants. Promotion to the rank of Major and beyond in the Infantry and Cavalry was made personally by the Emperor. In the Artillery, selection for promotion was done by the General of Artillery, and for the Frontier Units, the Grenzer, the officers were selected by the Supreme War Council (Hof Kriegsrath).

Austrian Generals were usually old and mostly aristocrats who had reached such exalted rank through their Court connections and intrigues. The losses of Austrian Generals in battle were much lower than the French, and even less than the Prussians and Russians. The type of campaign they fought was a defensive one, they worried too much about their lines of communication. The Archduke Charles said "Our Generals are the Army's greatest weakness". At Austerlitz, the battle plan drawn up by General Weyrother brought disaster to the Allied forces.

The Austrian Emperor with his Personal Guard
Previous page: Austrian Grenadiers

Austrian Infantry was divided in two groups, the Germans and the Hungarians. The former were renown for being better trained while the latter were well known for their fighting spirit, particularly the grenadiers.

The Light Infantry composed of Tyrolean sharpshooters, (Jäger), consisted of 200 companies from 50 to 200 men. Each one of these men was a hunter in civilian life and thus a very good shot.

The frontier units or Grenzer were historically composed of Christian refugees from the areas on the Austro-Turkish military border in the Balkans. Although they were classified as a militia, the High Command thought of them as something in between Light Infantry and Line Infantry.

In time of war, each Grenzer Regiment had 2 or 3 battalions, one of which always stayed behind to defend the frontier against the Turks. The Grenzer usually lacked uniforms and weapons and their military discipline was not very good. However, in battle they were excellent, and at Austerlitz, while the Regular troops fled the field, the Grenzer continued to fight, suffering some 70% casualties by the end of the battle.

The French soldiers considered the Grenzer as some of the best troops in the Austrian Army. After the further defeat of Austria in 1809, she ceded territory and 6 Grenzer regiments to France. These soldiers served Napoleon loyally until 1814.

Foto below: *The Austrian Infantryman was well equipped, each soldier carried a leather backpack which contained his belongings. There was a tent issued for every 5 soldiers, and a transport cart assigned for every company. There were an extra 4 to 6 carts and 30 mules to transport the battalion's ammunition.*

Above: *The Infantry uniform was white, the coat buttoned down the front from the collar to the waist. The German Regiments had white trousers and black gaiters, the Hungarian Regiments had light blue trousers with yellow cords and did not wear gaiters. In winter the great coats were white, brown or light grey.*

Below left: *The first and second rank Jägers were armed with smoothbore fusils, while the best shots in the third rank had rifles. The Non-commissioned officers also carried rifles, and each man carried 100 cartridges instead of the regulation 60 for infantry. The Jäger battalions formed part of Light Divisions and protected the Line Infantry or they acted independently.*
The quality of Austrian Light troops varied, but in general terms they were not better than the French Light troops. The incorrect use of these sharpshooters by the Austrian High command denied the Austrian Army the advantage the Jäger could bring to an Army executing an offensive or defensive manoeuvre. By 1810, changes in the training and the use of sharpshooters meant that by the campaigns of 1813-14 they were used in an efficiently on the battlefield.

Below left: *In 1805 the Austrian Army had 305 Line Regiments, 3 Jäger and 51 Grenzer battalions. They also had 20 Garrison battalions, 61 Reserve battalions, 12 Tyrolean Militia battalions and 12 Volunteer Jäger units. An Austrian battalion was the largest of any European Army at the time, it numbered 1,200 men, while a French battalion was 840 strong. The Jägers had a light blue-grey uniform, and wore black gaiters.*

The Austrian battle line formation was three ranks, at a distance of a single pace between each one. Until 1805 the Austrian regulations stated that the front rank had to be on its knees, but from 1805 onwards the front rank started to fire standing up. Archduke Charles ordered the infantry to cease firing when the enemy reached a distance of 40 meters and prepared to receive them with the bayonet. This order is in contrast to other European Armies of the time, particularly the British Army, which waited for the enemy to get very close before unleashing a storm of lead upon them. Scwarzenberg, on the other hand, preferred to use attack columns, sending a solid block of troops straight at the enemy protected by Light Infantry. Austrian infantry moved at speeds of 90, 105 or 120 paces per minute, depending on the terrain and the situation.

Above and centre: *Each soldier was armed with musket, a triangular bayonet and a sabre, as well as a cartridge box with 60 cartridges. The best shots were to be found amongst the Jäger and the Grenzer.*
In battle the Austrian Infantry used the typical formations of the time, just like any other European Army, that is lines, columns and squares as well as open order for the Light Infantry.

Below: *When engaged by cavalry, the infantry formed a Battalion Mass instead of a square of 3 files per side, as the Austrian Generals believed that such a formation would be too weak to withstand the onslaught of a French cavalry charge. The battalion mass was a column of a company width and six companies in depth. The mass could maneuver, but it was slow. These formations were vulnerable to artillery. If infantry was exposed to intense artillery fire they were ordered to lie down instead of remaining standing up as this reduced the casualty rate, but if the French had a lot of cavalry on the field this tactic would not work.*

Above and below: *The grenadiers were the elite of the Infantry, they were noticeable by their height, their mustaches and their fur caps. To be selected to be a grenadier an infantryman had to have 5 years service, and one campaign, he had to have proven valour and also be a good shot. Each battalion had 2 companies of grenadiers, the best soldiers of the whole battalion. Sometimes the companies were detached from the battalion and banded together with other grenadier companies to form Grenadier battalions.*

Centre: *Grenadiers wore a fur cap, 30 cm tall in the front and 12.5 cm in the back, with a brass plate on the front.*

Austrian cavalry included cuirassiers, Dragoons, Light Dragoons, Hussar and Uhlans (lancers). They were well trained and equipped, and they also had a very good reputation throughout Europe. However they had two weaknesses. First, there were not enough of them, generally the French had more cavalry than the Austrians on the battlefield; and second, they suffered from a rigid tactical doctrine that prevented them from operating effectively in groups larger than one or two cavalry regiments. The lack of precise instructions concerning the formation and handling of large bodies of cavalry in battle reduced the Austrian Cavalry's combat efficiency as did the tendency to place small units widely separated from each other. This meant that Austrian regiments and brigades were usually defeated by French brigades and divisions respectively.

Each regiment had 2 to 4 Divisions, each one formed of 2 squadrons. Each squadron had 6 officers, 14 non-commissioned officers and 150 troopers. According to the Austrian Regulations, the Division and not the squadron was the principal tactical unit.

The Light Dragoons had green uniforms and also had a leather helmet. They were armed with a carbine and a curved sabre. Each squadron had 16 men armed with rifles.

60 and 61: *The hussars had grey overalls with buttons down the side and leather reinforcement. The jacket, called a dolman, was decorated in the Hungarian style and on top of this jacket another one, called a pelisse was worn, usually fastened over one shoulder. The boots were cut in the traditional Hungarian style. They were armed with a curved sabre and a carbine, hussar model 1798.*

Above: *The Uhlans (lancers) wore a green jacket with red plastrons. Their trousers were green with red stripes down the side and they had leather reinforcements on the bottom of the leg. On campaign they could wear grey overalls. They were armed with 2 pistols, a curved sabre and a lance. The pennants on the laces were black over yellow. Each squadron had 8 men armed with rifles and 8 with carbines.*

Below: *The Cuirassiers used white uniforms, although on active service they could wear grey overalls instead of their white trousers. The boots reached the knees and the leather helmet had the Emperor's cypher, "FI" on a brass plate on the front. The troopers had to have short hair, the sideburns were not supposed to grow longer than the earlobe and all had to grow a moustache. The officers were not allowed to grow mustaches. Cuirassiers were armed with 2 pistols and a long straight bladed sword. They wore armor in the shape of a breast plate. Each squadron of cuirassiers had 8 men armed with rifles and 8 with carbines.*
Dragoons wore white uniforms and a leather helmet with a fur crest, which could be detached during a campaign. They were armed with carbines and a straight bladed sword. Each squadron had 16 men armed with rifles.

The Austrian Artillery had an excellent reputation for professionalism. It had gunpowder and ammunition of a better quality than the French. The Austrian Horse Artillery batteries transported the artillerymen who sat on the caissons and the cannons instead of on horseback. This made the artillery piece very sklow moving but it did offer one advantage... it took very little time to get the cannon into action. The Austrians also needed fewer horses and occupied less space on the field, making it a smaller target for the enemy gunners.

The French tended to use their artillery in an aggressive and imaginative manner, unlike the Austrians. All Austrian Artillerymen were volunteers, had signed up for 14 years and could read and write German.

Page 63: *The Austrian gun carriages were painted ochre, and the metal parts were in black. The ammunition wagons and caissons were painted yellow. A 6 pound gun (each shot weighed 3kg) had 94 round shot and 26 rounds of canister in the ammunition wagon. A 12 pound gun had 123 round shot, 40 canister and 12 grapeshot in the wagon. The remainder of the ammunition was kept in the Reserve Artillery Park. A 3 pound gun had a crew of 4 trained artillerymen and 4 assistants. A 12 pound gun had an NCO, 5 artillerymen and 9 assistants.*

Acknowledgements

Mr. Manuel Santiago Arenas Roca
Mr. Antonio Osende Barallobre,
Mr. Ronald Brighouse
Mr. Miguel Ángel Martín Más